MUSINGS

A SUITE FOR PIANO

by Ronald Bennett

Dedicated to
Gayle Spradley Bizzell, director of keyboard studies at Odessa College (Odessa, TX)
and her students

ISBN 978-1-4950-9287-9

WILLIS MUSIC

EXCLUSIVELY DISTRIBUTED BY

HAL•LEONARD®

7777 W. BLUEMOUND RD. P.O. BOX 13819 MILWAUKEE, WI 53213

Visit Hal Leonard Online at
www.halleonard.com

Friskiness

Ronald Bennett

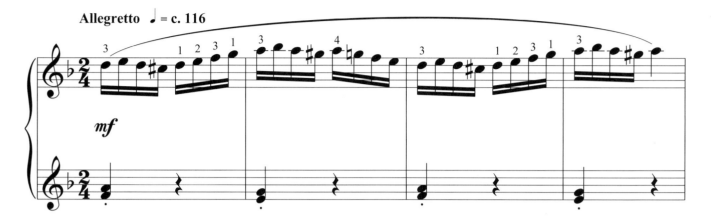

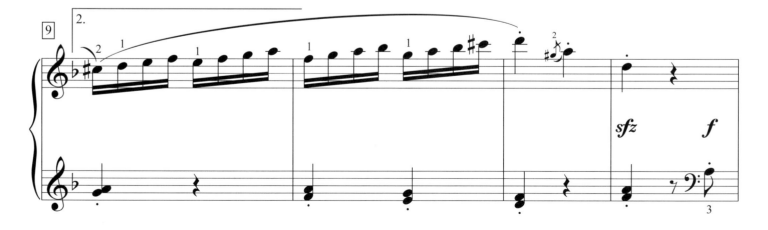

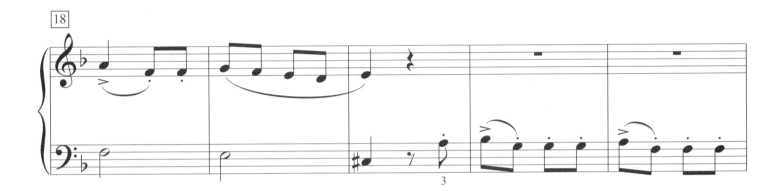

D.C. al Coda
(with repeat)

Apprehension

Ronald Bennett

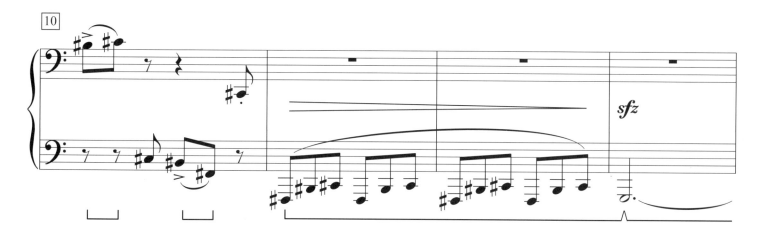

freely without measure, a la cadenza

flutter pedal

p *a tempo*   *mp*   *mf*

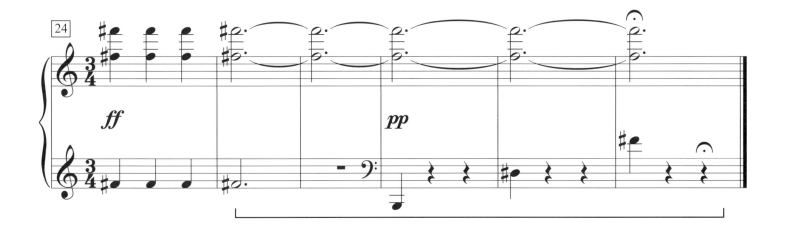

ff   *pp*

Exaltation

Ronald Bennett

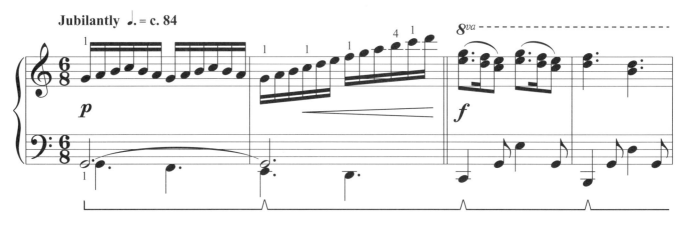

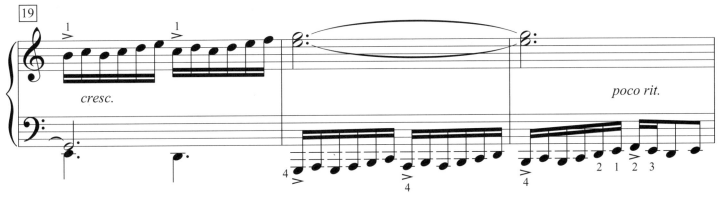

Contemplation
(Homage to Edward MacDowell)

Ronald Bennett

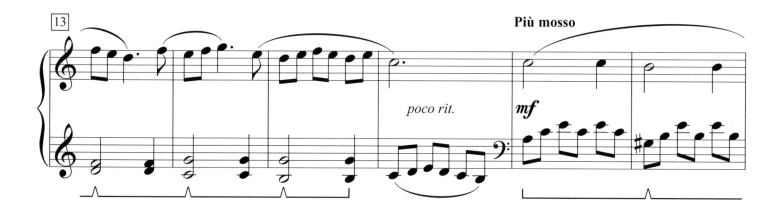

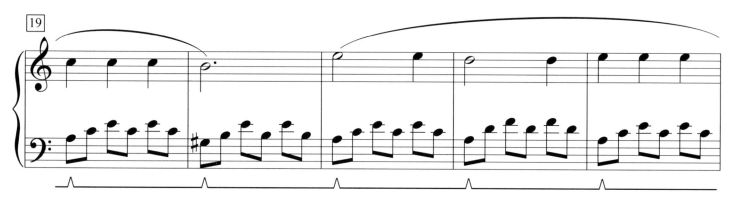

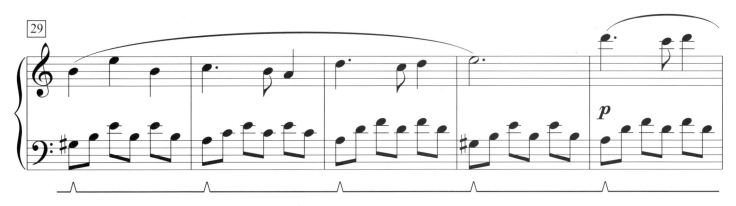

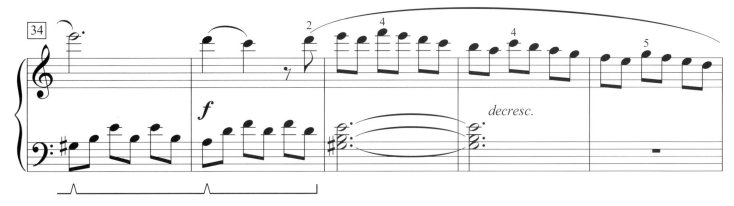

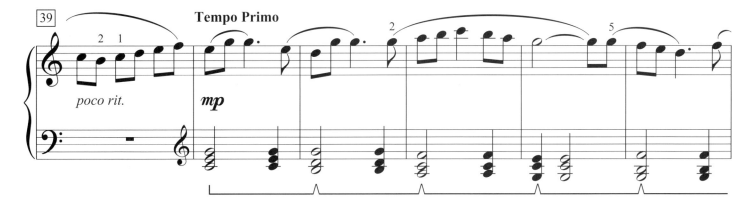

Busyness

Ronald Bennett

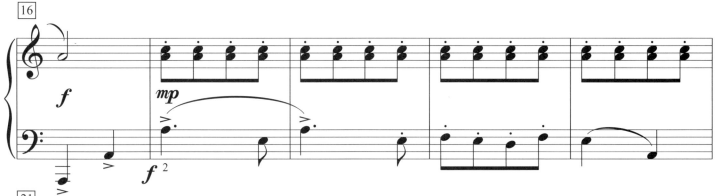

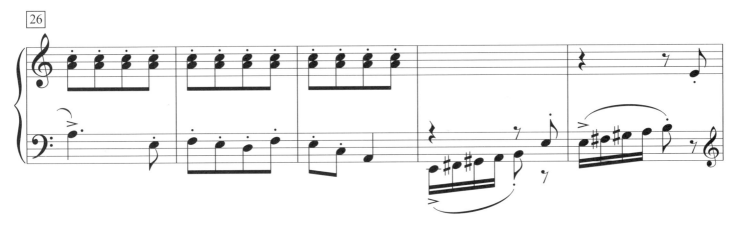

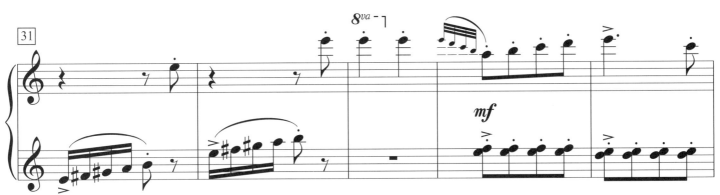

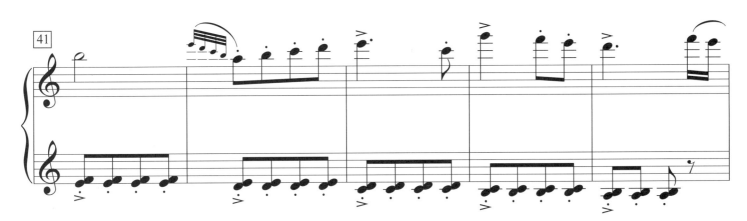

Satisfaction

Ronald Bennett

Andantino ♩ = c. 72

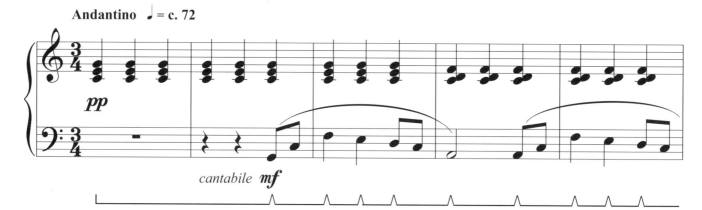

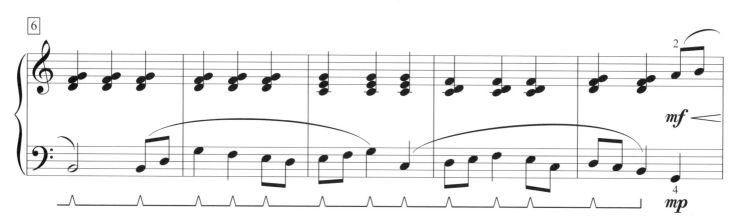

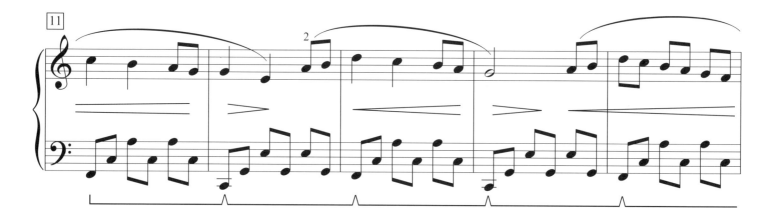

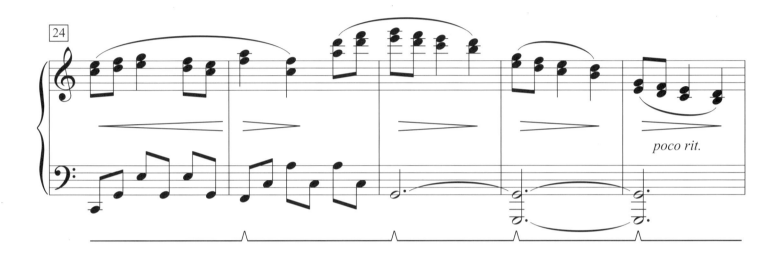

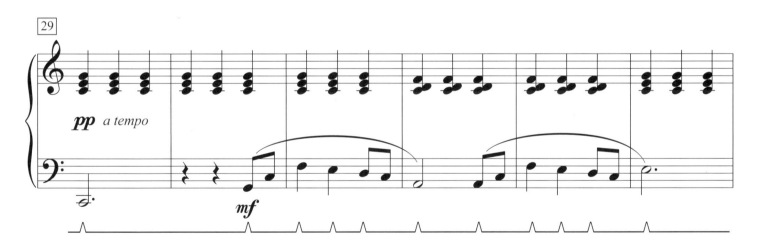

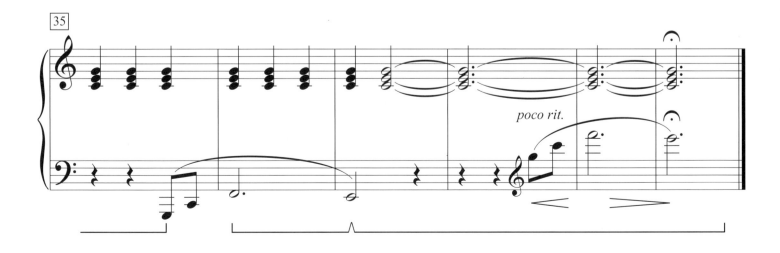

Vengeance

Ronald Bennett

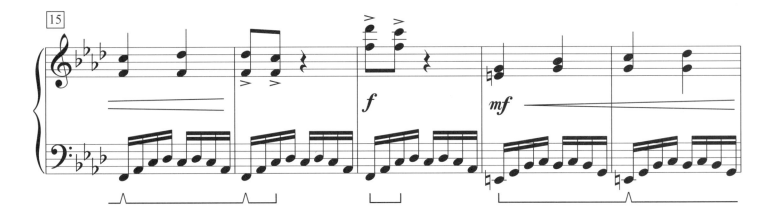

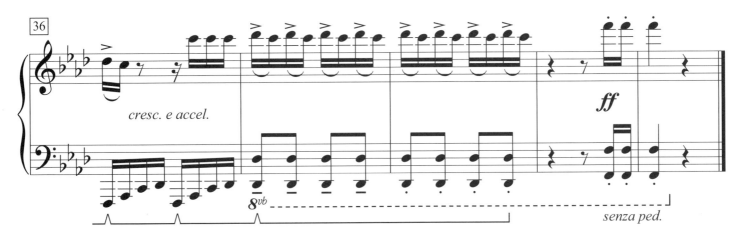

CLASSICAL PIANO SOLOS

Original Keyboard Pieces from Baroque to the 20th Century

Compiled and edited by Philip Low, Sonya Schumann, and Charmaine Siagian

First Grade

22 pieces: *Bartók*: A Conversation • *Mélanie Bonis*: Miaou! Ronron! • *Burgmüller*: Arabesque • *Handel*: Passepied • *d'Indy*: Two-Finger Partita • *Köhler*: Andantino • *Müller*: Lyric Etude • *Ryba*: Little Invention • *Schytte*: Choral Etude; Springtime • *Türk*: I Feel So Sick and Faint, and more!

00119738 / $6.99

Second Grade

22 pieces: *Bartók*: The Dancing Pig Farmer • *Beethoven*: Ecossaise • *Bonis*: Madrigal • *Burgmüller*: Progress • *Gurlitt*: Etude in C • *Haydn*: Dance in G • *d'Indy*: Three-Finger Partita • *Kirnberger*: Lullaby in F • *Mozart*: Minuet in C • *Petzold*: Minuet in G • *Purcell*: Air in D Minor • *Rebikov*: Limping Witch Lurking • *Schumann*: Little Piece • *Schytte*: A Broken Heart, and more!

00119739 / $6.99

Third Grade

20 pieces: *CPE Bach*: Presto in C Minor • *Bach/Siloti*: Prelude in G • *Burgmüller*: Ballade • *Cécile Chaminade*: Pièce Romantique • *Dandrieu*: The Fifers • *Gurlitt*: Scherzo in D Minor • *Hook*: Rondo in F • *Krieger*: Fantasia in C • *Kullak*: Once Upon a Time • *MacDowell*: Alla Tarantella • *Mozart*: Rondino in D • *Rebikov*: Playing Soldiers • *Scarlatti*: Sonata in G • *Schubert*: Waltz in F Minor, and more!

00119740 / $7.99

Fourth Grade

18 pieces: *CPE Bach*: Scherzo in G • *Teresa Carreño*: Berceuse • *Chopin*: Prelude in E Minor • *Gade*: Little Girls' Dance • *Granados*: Valse Poetic No. 6 • *Grieg*: Arietta • *Handel*: Prelude in G • *Heller*: Sailor's Song • *Kuhlau*: Sonatina in C • *Kullak*: Ghost in the Fireplace • *Moszkowski*: Tarentelle • *Mozart*: Allegro in G Minor • *Rebikov*: Music Lesson • *Satie*: Gymnopedie No. 1 • *Scarlatti*: Sonata in G • *Telemann*: Fantasie in C, and more!

00119741 / $7.99

Fifth Grade

19 pieces: *Bach*: Prelude in C-sharp Major • *Beethoven:* Moonlight sonata • *Chopin*: Waltz in A-flat • *Cimarosa*: Sonata in E-flat • *Coleridge-Taylor*: They Will Not Lend Me a Child • *Debussy*: Doctor Gradus • *Grieg*: Troldtog • *Griffes*: Lake at Evening • *Lyadov*: Prelude in B Minor • *Mozart*: Fantasie in D Minor • *Rachmaninoff*: Prelude in C-sharp Minor • *Rameau*: Les niais de Sologne • *Schumann:* Farewell • *Scriabin*: Prelude in D, and more!

00119742 / $8.99

The *Classical Piano Solos* series offers carefully-leveled, original piano works from Baroque to the early 20th century, featuring the simplest classics in Grade 1 to concert-hall repertoire in Grade 5. An assortment of pieces are featured, including familiar masterpieces by Bach, Beethoven, Mozart, Grieg, Schumann, and Bartók, as well as several lesser-known works by composers such as Melanie Bonis, Anatoly Lyadov, Enrique Granados, Vincent d'Indy, Theodor Kullak, and Samuel Coleridge-Taylor.

- Grades 1-4 are presented in a suggested order of study. Grade 5 is laid out chronologically.

- Features clean, easy-to-read engravings with clear but minimal editorial markings.

- View complete repertoire lists of each book along with sample music pages at **www.willispianomusic.com**.

The series was compiled to loosely correlate with the *John Thompson Modern Course*, but can be used with any method or teaching situation.

EXCLUSIVELY DISTRIBUTED BY
HAL•LEONARD®

Willis Piano Music

Willis Piano

Willis Piano

0517